Plain Talk About the Pastorate
Roy W. Hinchey

Broadman Press
Nashville, Tennessee

4224-10
ISBN: 0-8054-2410-5

Dewey Decimal Classification: 254
Subject Headings: MINISTERS
Printed in the United States of America

Foreword

There has been a growing concern in recent years on the part of Baptists for ministers needing assistance in locating fields of service and for churches needing assistance in finding pastors. This concern led the Georgia Baptist Convention in 1970 to authorize the establishment of a Church-Minister Relations Service as a phase of the state mission program.

The Rev. Roy W. Hinchey, at that time pastor of the Jefferson Avenue Baptist Church, of East Point, Georgia, was elected in the fall of 1971 as the first secretary of the newly established ministry. Brother Hinchey began in an uncharted area, but one for which he was exceedingly well qualified by temperament, training, and experience.

Mr. Hinchey is the son of a Baptist minister and is a graduate of Carson-Newman College and the Southern Baptist Theological Seminary. He served successfully for over thirty years in pastorates in Tennessee and Georgia. Through those years, he was active in denominational work. Denominational service included terms as vice-president of the Tennessee and Georgia conventions and moderator of the Atlanta Baptist Association.

In authorizing the new Church-Minister Relations Service, the Georgia Baptist Convention stated specifically: "The proposed service . . . will be available to both churches and ministers upon a request basis only, and that the principles of the sovereignty of Christ, the leadership of the Holy Spirit, and the autonomy of the church, and the freedom and responsibility of both ministers and churches will be respected."

The Executive Committee stipulated further that the secretary of Church-Minister Relations Service was not to become involved in "church and denominational politics," but he was to serve both ministers and churches in the spirit of Christ.

The Holy Spirit surely led in the call of Brother Hinchey to the new field of work, for he more than met the expectations stated by the Convention and the Executive Committee. With compassionate concern and wisdom he served, and increasingly his guidance and council was sought. In a period of three years he served several hundred persons and churches, and made sure the foundations and indicated the direction this new ministry among Southern Baptists should take.

Brother Hinchey has been called upon frequently to share his insights and convictions concerning the work of the ministry. His messages in the churches, pastors' conferences, associational meetings, and articles in various denominational journals have strengthened pastors and the churches. Broadman Press is rendering a service in publishing this book which makes available to a much larger audience the wisdom of one who has proven to be a good minister of Jesus Christ and a helpful counselor to brother ministers and leaders in the churches.

I welcome the opportunity to express appreciation and affection for the author and to commend the book, *Plain Talk About the Pastorate.*

SEARCY S. GARRISON
Executive Secretary-Treasurer
Executive Committee,
Georgia Baptist Convention

Preface

As secretary of Church-Minister Relations Service of the Georgia Baptist Convention, I have addressed many pastors' conferences over the state, and these chapters are based largely upon these addresses.

Usually the addresses were followed by a question-and-answer period and general discussion. It was found that pastors were more free to discuss their problems than formerly. That is good because pastors themselves are their own most effective teachers. My purpose here is to share some of those discussions with other pastors. As we helped one another, perhaps this book can help still others. I apologize for making frequent use of "I." This seeming egotism may be softened because some of the ideas have come from thirty-eight years in the pastorate including some denominational work. Any other expression might strain honesty.

If some burdened and discouraged minister can be strengthened, I will have adequate reward.

I am greatly indebted to Miss Lucy Justus, staff writer for the *Atlanta Journal-Constitution Magazine*, for typing the manuscript.

ROY W. HINCHEY

**Dedicated
To my father
Rev. George Henry Hinchey
who taught me most
about Christ**

Contents

Contents

1
Tensions of
the Modern Minister

It was Monday morning and the pastors' conference was in session. The time had come for announcements and introductions. Seriously, but with a touch of humor, a pastor got up and said, "Fellows, you know that congregation voted my pulpit vacant with me standing right in it."

He smiled when he said it. The others smiled, but it could be classified as grim humor. Every pastor was made fully aware that he occupied a very vulnerable position. In other days when ministers made their living farming or by carpentry, teaching, or other means, it might not be so serious. In our complicated existence it could bring want and disaster.

Shock, frustration, change, collapse, crisis, are words that have had increasing meaning in our time. Books entitled *The Lonely Crowd, The Affluent Society, The Other America, Future Shock* reflect some of the general tensions among us. We read of "psychedelic churches," "free" universities, science cities in the Arctics, marital tribes, and strange religious cults. We have been frightened by the threatened population explosion and the knowledge explosion.

Ministers are not the only ones who have felt the shock of change. We are a moving people. Alvin Toffler reminds us that the average American in 1914 traveled about 340 miles per year by aid of horse or mechanical means. Today the average American car owner will drive at least 10,000 miles per year.[1] We "use up" space rapidly and throw it away.

The minister can hardly remain unaffected by this changing, rapidly moving society. Although he is not alone in his frustrations and anxieties, there are tensions peculiar to his profession.

Most ministers do not like to discuss this phase of their life—especially the possibility that their pulpit might be "voted vacant." They think, "Oh, well, it couldn't happen to me." Yet there remains that haunting uneasiness, particularly after a minister passes the age of 45. The causes and blame are matters for debate. The truth remains that it does sometimes happen to a good man. Those of us who have escaped cannot assume a superior role and say, "We are better than you." Paul got kicked out of a few places.

It can be especially disastrous to an older man. He may have spent twenty-five years or more in the ministry. He is trained for nothing else. He cannot go out and get another church like one would get another job. If he applies for a pastorate directly, he is turned off. The church thinks something is wrong. There is that agonizing uncertainty that comes with waiting. He has no unemployment insurance and often no savings.

He is not the only one who suffers. There is his family and children. The church suffers; sometimes it is difficult to call another pastor because they are "split." Some members will be against anyone called because they feel the former pastor was not treated right. Sometimes the right pastor will not accept because he feels it could happen to him.

There are other tensions and pressures that do not come from the laity. These are built up on the inside of the pastor himself. He may feel he is not a success unless he gets appointed to a certain board or elected to a coveted position. He forgets that the limelight does not always spell success.

Some pastors were talking one Monday morning. One

said, "I had 1,015 in Sunday School." Another said, "I had 12 additions, 8 by baptism." The third was silent. One of the two with pride showing through asked the third pastor, "What kind of day did you have?" He blushed and finally answered, "We had some wonderful prayers." Only God can determine who had the greatest day.

There are the pressures of youth. Youth are under pressure and sometimes they exert pressure. They have been saying, "Let's change the church and do it now. If necessary, fire the old crowd and start over." Do it by revolution. Christ is sometimes pictured as a militant revolutionary. Sometimes the pastor gets caught in the line of fire.

There need not be a generation gap that promotes hostility. The church needs all ages and each age has a contribution to offer. Someone put it like this, "Choose all young men for deacons and you will blow up; choose all old men and you will dry up; mix them up and you will grow up." There is sense in that statement, but the fact remains that it is not always heeded. And that adds to the tensions of the pastor.

There are family pressures. Churches are tempted to expect too much of the pastor's family. Sometimes pastors expect too much of their families because others do. A woman said, "Our pastor's son has hair like a hippie." What is the Christian course to follow when a pastor discovers that his teenage daughter is to become an unwed mother? Shall he seek the rehabilitation of his daughter or first try to preserve his image as example to the flock? Situations like this occur in our permissive society. The church is not always charitable and redemptive in its attitude.

The pastor's wife comes in for her share. She is expected to be a model mother and housekeeper. Some expect her to attend all the meetings but not say too much. She is expected to know the answers but has no title. Like her husband, she is placed in an impossible role. The pastor feels the pressure placed on his wife.

Perhaps the greatest tensions come because of the role in which the pastor sees himself and the role the congregation expects of him. He is not given a specific job description. He has no specified hours, but he is expected to always be on duty. Often pastor selection committees do not bother to explain to the prospective pastor what the church expects of him. He is just told to preach the gospel and visit. The word "ministry" has become a nebulous term. It can mean different things to different people, and it does.

Salary is another source of tension for the pastor. The rapid rise of inflation has brought complications. A pastor is expected to dress well, travel well, keep up with current knowledge, and be acceptable to all kinds of people. His expenses are above those of the average family, but he is expected to do all these things on an average salary or less. Often he cannot get by without his wife working or he gets an extra job. As the years pile up, he wonders how he will educate his children and how he will provide for his retirement.

In the midst of these tensions, some will not be able to cope. Some will drop out. Others will not drop out but will become so disillusioned they will be ineffective in their ministry and be "left out." On the surface the picture is dark. It is estimated that 1,000 Southern Baptist pastors leave the ministry every year.[2] The same problem is prevalent in every major denomination in this country. About 10,000 priests and clergymen of all denominations leave the ministry each year according to a survey.

A professor in a large interdenominational black seminary believes that the problem of dropouts is not so acute among his students. Black pastors feel little if any inhibition from their congregations on entering social movements. This fact, the professor believes, may have kept some from leaving the ministry. A study made of the students in this school indicated that 90 percent wanted to enter the pastoral ministry.

What is the answer? Where are we heading? Perhaps we would do well to look at the present and future in light of Christian history. Ministers have always hurt. There are times when there is no way to avoid it. The ancient prophets hurt. Jeremiah cried out, "Oh that my head were waters, and mine eyes a fountain of tears, that I might weep day and night for the slain of the daughters of my people!" He went on to say, "Oh that I had in the wilderness a lodging place of wayfaring men; that I might leave my people, and go from them! for they be all adulterers, an assembly of treacherous men" (Jer. 9:1-2). It sounds like he was ready to quit the ministry!

Jesus hurt. We must never forget that even though he had a sunny disposition he was "acquainted with grief." He was as thoroughly human as he was divine. He was painfully aware of the frailty of his followers. We read that "many of his disciples went back, and walked no more with him." Wistfully, he turned to the twelve and asked, "Will ye also go away?" (see John 6:66-67).

All the great leaders of our Christian faith have had moments of despair. Perhaps the solution to our problem lies in the way Jesus handled his. He hurt but he used his hurts in a redemptive sense. Paul hurt but he rejoiced that his hurts turned out for the "furtherance of the gospel" (Phil. 1:12). His trials did not crush him. They refined him. Iron must go through the fire before it becomes steel. God does not take us out of the battle; he does something better. He gives us the strength we need.

The pastor, like his Master, "does not come to call the righteous but sinners to repentance." He should heed the admonition of Jesus: "They that be whole need not a physician, but they that are sick" (Matt. 9:12). The physician is not immune to the diseases he treats. The pastor is physician to the sin-sick. Like the physician, he is not immune to the disease that infects his flock. Often he must go himself to the Great Physician, to whom he refers his members, for his own personal healing. Sometimes he will need the healing help of his peers. Denominational leaders and laymen are becoming aware of this. Some will find after a try that they can serve God more effectively in avenues other than the pastoral ministry. They should not feel inferior or demoted if they face the issue frankly and change course. In spite of the anguish, worry, apathy, bewilderment, fear, and anxiety, others will go on and find strength as they go.

The minister must not counsel long with his fears. He must look up in faith. When I was a young pastor an older colleague said to me, "I don't envy you. My ministry is about over. I would dread to start in these times." I do not feel that way. I believe God is about to do the biggest things he has done since Christ's first coming. It is our job to find out what he is doing and help him all we can.

1. Alvin Toffler, *Future Shock* (New York: Bantam Books, Inc., 1970), pp. 75-76.
2. Jim Newton, "The Uneasy Pulpit," *Home Missions*, June, 1974, pp. 16-17.

2
The Tap on
the Shoulder

That's what Peter Marshall called it. He spoke of "God's nugatory influences" [1] in his life. He had some close brushes with death. These experiences gave him a sense of destiny and purpose. But "nugatory forces" were not all that influenced him. Once he heard a missionary speak. The missionary was not seeking money but recruits. The appeal deeply touched the young man. At the close of the meeting he publicly stated that he accepted the missionary's challenge. "I have determined," he said, "to give my life to God for him to use me wherever he wants me."

One morning a man just starting the study of medicine attended an associational meeting of churches. He heard A. M. Poindexter preach. In the message, the preacher spoke of consecrating one's wealth, mental gifts, and possible attainments to the work of the ministry. He held up the thought that great sacrifice and toil would be paid a hundredfold by being the instrument of saving one soul. After the message, young John A. Broadus found his pastor. He said, "Brother Grimsley, the question is decided; I must try to be a preacher." [2]

In a revival meeting, a pastor stood to give his testimony. "There has never been a time in my memory when I did not want to be a preacher," he said. He went on to explain that as a boy even, before he became a church member, he felt the "tap on the shoulder." There was no dramatic experience but he was sure of his destiny.

A well-known contemporary pastor said, "Actually from

the time I was a very little boy, I have had something of the sense of a call to preach." [3] He was converted at the age of seven but said, "I can distinctly remember a conscious desire to be a minister of the gospel before my conversion."

Other men have felt the call later in life. My father was in his late thirties when he was ordained. He continuously served rural churches until he was eighty-two. One didn't retire in those days. He always said his call to preach was as real as his conversion.

I have not related these experiences to suggest that everyone in the ministry should have the same experiences. There is reality in a divine call, but every call is not dramatic and instantaneous. Some have worried because they have not had a Pauline experience. They have seen no bright lights and heard no voices. I saw no lights. I heard no voices. It was real, but it was gradual. Perhaps it is time for us to rethink the biblical concept of a call to the ministry.

There is a sense in which all Christians are called. God takes the initiative in salvation. Jesus said that he came to call "sinners to repentance" (Matt. 9:13). That is probably the first meaning of the call. This call summons all the redeemed to full-time Christian service. This is an important biblical doctrine. Elton Trueblood said, "The Christian groceryman must give full time, just as the clergyman does—his major time being given in his store." [4] Pastors and staff members have no right to glory in the contrast between their status and that of ordinary Christians. Egocentricity has no place here. We have no natural right to accept obeisance. It is foreign to the New Testament picture. Jesus took a towel, girded himself, and washed his disciples' feet.

Paul said, "There are diversities of gifts, but the same Spirit" (1 Cor. 12:4). Some are gifted in preaching, others in teaching. Others serve best by means of deeds, visiting, helping the helpless, feeding the hungry. An invitation to full-time Christian service that every Christian could accept would not be out of place in a worship service. We will remain weak as long as we reserve the call exclusively to professional Christian vocations.

We recognize the call of God to all Christians for full-time service. At the same time we must not negate the call to specialized Christian ministries. That call is also scriptural. You will note that people in the early church were identified not by the offices they held but by the spiritual gifts they exercised. There was little formal structure. As time passed, some structure was needed and some offices. We find the terms "bishop," "elder," and "deacon." This tended to make a distinction between laity and clergy. The distinction, however, was not in terms of superiority. It was based on the service they rendered. Gradually the clergy became superior in the eyes of the church. It is difficult to believe that Christ meant it that way. The difference is in the need they meet rather than the superiority of their office.

But if men are called into special services for Christ, how can they know it? It might help to eliminate the idea that everyone must have a Pauline experience. It must have been great for him, but there was only one Paul. Even in the Bible, experiences similar to that are unique. Many of the early disciples responded to the simple words "Follow me." They were called in the midst of the ordinary rather than the spectacular. Walking by the Sea of Galilee, Jesus saw two brothers straining at a net, trying to cast it into the sea. He said, "Follow me, and I will make you fishers of men" (Matt. 4:19). Matthew heard the call of Christ in a tax office. The call came in the midst of the complaints of people over their tax bills. So you see you are not alone if you do not have a dramatic experience. Who would dare say that the call of men like Matthew, Peter, James, and

John was not real? Yet there were no bright lights. No unearthly voices. No signs in the sky.

God speaks in many different ways and in many languages. Sometimes he speaks to us through an emotion. His voice can be heard in a prayer, a song, or a sermon. The words may not be audible. He may not be visible, but his will is definitely perceived.

God gave us emotions. He gave us intellect. I believe both should be used. They should both be used in determining his will for our lives. I like the way the mountain preacher expressed it. He said, "If God had not intended for us to use our heads, he might have put feet on both ends of us." It is as important to use your head as your heart.

In determining the will of God for your life, it is important to take a close look at your natural endowments. They are gifts of God. It seems too much to assume that God would call a person to a task and not give him the ability to do the task. The ability may be latent, but if it is not there you may well question the validity of the call. We cannot keep from wondering if this does not explain the "drop out" of some ministers. God does not expect us to strain beyond our reach.

It may take a spiritual struggle to reach a definite conclusion. After one has evaluated his perception of God's will, his feelings, and his God-given endowments, the battle is still not over. His will must be brought into action. He must will to do God's will, and he must will to do his best.

I believe a call to serve God in the ministry is a call to prepare. Leading a church is not easy. Preaching God's message Sunday after Sunday calls for a thorough knowledge of the Bible. It requires knowledge in many other realms. God will give us wisdom if we ask for it, but he will not give us knowledge. We must sweat for it. One time I was told by a well-meaning person not to study for an examination. This person said, "Pray about it, and go to church, and you will pass." I tried it, and it didn't come out that way! God will not do our "homework" for us. I believe a minister should get the best training possible. Somewhere along the way he will find a use for most of the real truth he can learn. He will especially need to master the rules of language. Few congregations today will tolerate a minister who mutilates the English language. In this day of opportunity, there is no excuse for it. Many men who never had the opportunity of attending seminary have become masters in the use of language and communication.

Although the final decision must be made at the altar in one's own soul, it is wise to listen to the counsel of Christian friends. Usually God convinces others that one is called. I will never forget the encouragement given by the humble Christians in the rural church I attended as a boy. Knowing me as they did, many frankly said, "We believe God wants you to be a preacher." The pastor put it this way, "If you can't be sure, don't." I will be forever grateful to them and to him.

1. Catherine Marshall, *A Man Called Peter* (New York: Avon Books, The Hearst Corp., 1951), p. 24.

2. Archibald Thomas Robertson, *The Life and Letters of John A. Broadus* (Philadelphia: American Baptist Publishing Society, 1910), p. 53.

3. Harper Shannon, *Trumpets in the Morning* (Nashville: Broadman Press, 1969), p. 15.

4. Elton Trueblood, *The Company of the Committed* (New York: Harper & Row, 1961), p. 59.

3
Joy in
the Ministry

I have enjoyed being a preacher. Some will object to the word "preacher." In Tennessee and Georgia where I grew up and where I served, the term is widely used, and it is a word of endearment. For that reason, I do not object to being addressed as "Preacher." I have been thrilled when I was introduced by a friend who said, "This is my preacher." From here on I will use the word "minister" or "pastor" because they are more widely accepted.

In the "turbulent sixties" many of us became alarmed. Seminary students were turning to avenues of ministry other than the pastorate. They were telling us that the church and the ministry were irrelevant. Ministers were given lower ratings than other professions in popular appeal. They were no longer the leading figures in the community. Some even went so far as to declare that a man of integrity could not be a minister.

Hopefully, I see a different trend. In interviewing numbers of seminary men in the last few years, I found the vast majority looking forward to the pastorate. They are seeing it in a different light. They recognize the hazards, but they also see the opportunities. The pastorate is where the action is. If churches are ever changed for the better, they will not be changed by suggestions or even directions given by high ecclesiastical offices. They will be changed by God-called pastors, preaching, teaching, and working among people day after day.

It will not be easy. There was a time when a man was

recognized and respected just because he was a minister. Along with the doctor, the teacher, and the lawyer, the minister was among the few people with college degrees. Now he has more competition. He is no longer generally respected just because of his calling. He *can* have, even now, as much respect as was accorded to the minister in other days, but there is a difference. He must earn it on his own. He must prove himself. The world is saying more frankly, "What do you have to offer?" Many pastors are making their lives felt in every area of community life. This wide influence does not come suddenly. It can come only after the people have seen and experienced the spirit and love of Christ in the minister.

I have enjoyed being a pastor because there are needs. People have needs that only a devoted pastor can fill. There comes a time when the skilled physician must turn away. There are avenues the legal profession dare not tread. Psychiatry can go only so far. There are doors open to the pastor which are not open to people in any other profession.

I will never forget one experience that brought joy to my heart and others. A teenage girl was in the hospital. She was suffering from nervous and physical disorder. She was in a serious depression. Her father asked me, her pastor, to visit her. I did. I found a serious emotional problem. Because of some former actions, she was convinced her father and brother did not love her. Her world was her family. That world had come apart in her own thinking, and she wanted to die.

I went to her father and said, "If this were my daughter, I would go in, put my arms around her and tell her I loved her and held no past actions against her. I'd also ask her brother to do the same." They followed these suggestions. The next day I visited her. I talked with her nurse. I was told that a marvelous change had come over her. She would soon be well enough to go home.

The dedicated pastor will find himself on many teams meeting human need. There are few pressures and needs in the community that do not finally come across his desk. He has the privilege in many communities of knocking on doors and saying, "I'm the pastor of the church. May I visit in your home a few minutes?" If he will not abuse this privilege and will go in the name of the Lord, he will find most doors open to him. I enjoy being among the people.

I enjoy being a minister because I have so many opportunities to introduce people to Jesus. Many times, I have let golden opportunities slip by. Many times I have suffered defeat. Even when I succeeded one time in a hundred, the joy overshadowed the defeats.

G. Campbell Morgan said, "I stand in the presence of an eternal ethical code such as that of Moses and I do not tremble. But whenever I come near the Incarnate Purity, into the presence of Incarnate Love, I am ashamed, debased, bowed in the dust." [1] Christ does convict us of sin, but he does not leave us bowed in the dust. He offers forgiveness, hope and reassurance. The Christian minister has the privilege of bringing to people the most heartening news that can be told.

We are told that in the early days of his ministry, Thomas Chalmers thundered against the grosser crimes of the people. He confessed later that he never heard of any reformation wrought among them. Not until he began to tell them of the free offer of forgiveness through the sacrifice of Christ did he note great changes among them. He learned that the preaching of Jesus Christ is the only effective way of preaching morality.

J. Wallace Hamilton said, "When I get too old to preach, just give me a corner in the church where I can talk to people, not in crowds, but one by one, as persons, for I have learned some things which I once believed, but now I know." [2] As the years have passed, I have experienced the force of his statement. I have seen Christ do for people what no one else could do. I once believed it. Now I know it. I have seen them come from the place of prayer with tears of joy and victory in their eyes. The world had not changed, but *they* had changed.

As a state secretary of Church-Minister Relations Service, I have listened to the heartaches, frustrations, failures, pressures, and family problems of many pastors. I have also seen joy in the faces of most of them as even in seeming defeat they were experiencing a more realistic sense of God's presence.

One day a drop-out pastor came to talk. At that time he was in secular work and earning a sizable income, far more than the average pastor. He told me of his work and discussed briefly his experience in his last pastorate. But something seemed to be lacking. After a pause, I asked, "Are you happy?" Quickly he answered, "No, I'm miserable and my wife is miserable. I want a church. That's why I'm here."

I warned him that it would be difficult for him to find a church where the salary would be anywhere near his present income. He said, "My wife and I have settled that matter. We are willing to serve where God wants us no matter what the cost."

God soon led this young man to a small but challenging church. He gave up his well-paying job and gladly accepted it. He will tell you quickly that there is joy in the ministry.

For nearly forty years, I have regularly attended pastors' conferences. Some were in large cities, others in rural areas. In all of these I saw the same general audience. Some were old men, eighty and beyond, yet eager to go on serving. There were also the young men, excited, vibrant, eager to get started. All these testify that the ministry is a rewarding and fulfilling way of life.

Experiences like these give me courage. We need not cower in a corner apologizing for our faith. We have found the "way." That way is Christ himself. It is the way to which all the world's people must some day come if they experience the fullness of life. That truth makes me enjoy being a minister.

1. G. Campbell Morgan, *Evangelism* (New York: Fleming H. Revell Co., 1904), p. 18.

2. J. Wallace Hamilton, *What About Tomorrow?* (Old Tappan, N.J.: Fleming H. Revell Co., 1972), p. 154.

4
How to
Be Miserable in
the Ministry

Why is it that some men carry the heavy burdens of a pastorate like they were feathers? Why do others reel and stagger, grumble and complain, making their companions miserable with them?

Perhaps there are as many answers as there are individuals. We are not all made from identical patterns. We do not all have the same spiritual and social backgrounds. Churches also differ. Most will agree that some charges are more difficult than others. A Texas preacher in his homespun way said, "Any horse in Texas can be rode but not every man can ride every horse." It is our conviction that every church can be shepherded, but not every man can shepherd every church. There are some basic attitudes, however, which are apparent too often among those who have found misery in the pastorate.

One of these attitudes is an overdose of self-esteem. A veteran minister said, "A man is in line for misery if in his own estimation he becomes too big to move down and in the estimation of others too little to step up."

Pride is the scriptural word here. It is listed among the "seven deadly sins" and it naturally comes first. We are warned that "pride goeth before destruction" (Prov. 16:18). This does not mean that God hates self-respect. It does not mean that he wants us to lose our sense of personal dignity. It does mean that station, rank, and prestige are not to be the goals of a minister of Jesus Christ.

Some men feel that if, by manipulation or pulling ecclesiastical strings, they can get called to a big church, they will be "big preachers." Nothing could be farther from the truth. It doesn't help the player or the game when a man gets out of his league. It is one way to find misery.

Others feel that when they move it must be to a bigger place or a bigger salary. A so-called "lateral" move would be unthinkable or disgraceful. Too often the end result is they stay when they should move, the church suffers, and they find misery.

We are not trying to say it is a sin to be prominent, even a celebrity. It is not a sin to hold a position of prestige. It becomes a sin when motives like these become our aim and dominating purpose. If they lurk in our hearts, God knows it, and the people we attempt to serve become aware of it. We could very easily class ourselves with those who "love the uppermost rooms at feasts, and the chief seats in the synagogues" (Matt. 23:6). Remember, Jesus said, "Whosoever shall exalt himself shall be abased; and he that shall humble himself shall be exalted" (Matt. 23:12). Our only glory is a reflected glory that comes from the Son of righteousness. We will be truly exalted as we reflect his life in word and deed. Some pastors have found promotion in their own church fields through hard work and complete commitment.

It is true that great responsibility brings greatness to the surface. It is also true that it will not bring it up if it is not there in the first place. One of the truly great pastors that I have known never occupied a prominent pulpit. He never preached a convention sermon. Yet he is known far and wide as a man of God. Pastors and laymen alike have turned to him in times of crisis.

Another way to be miserable is to concentrate on the faults and failures of the members of the church. This does not imply that we are to refrain from condemning sin. Even this, however, should be done in love. If it is not done in love, it will not correct the evil. It will only serve to alienate and build a wall between pastor and people. We have too many walls. Christ is a wall breaker.

I remember very distinctly an experience in my own ministry. I had become very discouraged. Some of my members were acting very unsaintly. One of my pet projects had failed. It was one of my blue Mondays or Fridays—I've forgotten which. I went home. While the family was out, I went into the kitchen to talk with Mother. As I sat there wrapped in gloom, I said, "Mother, I shouldn't have been a preacher. I should have stayed here and worked on the farm." I went on to relate all the misery I had experienced blow by blow.

Mother listened patiently as mothers are supposed to do, but she didn't coddle me. She treated me like a man. "Son," she said, "God didn't call you to preach to saints. He called you to preach to sinners. If they were all nice people, they wouldn't need you. Remember, Christ loved people. You have to learn to love people 'warts and all.' He did and you can. Now you just go back there and love those people no matter what they do, and let them see a little of God in you. That's what they need. You will also find they will return that love." It was a sermon I needed, and I've been trying to live by it since that day.

Sometimes we wonder how much our people love us, or if they love us at all. If we look into our own hearts to see how much we love them, we will not have to ask. We will find that they love us about as much as we love them.

A great pastor once said, "You never become pastor of a church until you come to love it more than your own life." Was he right? We can preach to them, exhort them, possibly teach them some needed truth. We will hardly be their pastor unless we love them enough to suffer with them and help bear their burdens. Jesus prayed, "As thou hast sent me into the world, even so have I also sent them into the world" (John 17:18). He made our position and our direction clear.

If you want to be truly miserable, you might try another route. Set up for yourself some worldly standards of success. In the business world a man is usually counted a success if he makes more sales and accumulates more capital than his competitors. The American dream is to reach the top of the heap. In the political world, the word is power.

In giving this warning there is a word of caution. It is a common trick of persons who have failed to get on in the world to assume an injured air of innocence. It is easy to complain of the world's injustice in conferring its honors on merely pushing men while they who have toiled honestly are neglected. God is not against success, and he is not against baptisms and budgets, or even buildings. Someone must have counted the converts at Pentecost and the hundred and twenty followers who came together to pray (see Acts 1:15; 2:41).

The difference between worldly and Godly success is in another area. The difference is in the source of power. The Pentecost story reminds us there is something other than what we see. "Simon Peter, the fisherman" is not the whole story at all. That something else is what we call "Spirit." He came into the degenerate Roman world like a mighty rushing wind and flames of fire. Institutions and ideas men thought were fixed forever began to change. This life-giving power came from outside.

If we are to be successful, we need the power of the same Spirit. It is the task of the church and its ministers to present opportunities for the Spirit to break through. If we do this, no power can keep us from being successful.

This success may not measure up (or down) to the standards of the world. It will cause others to take notice. Christ working through his people is as powerful today as he was in the first century. The pastor who is a channel through which the Spirit can flow is a success.

5
When Should a Pastor Leave?

Pastors sometimes speak of the first few months on the field as the "honeymoon." There is the reception, the round of invitations, and the joy of meeting new people. He goes to the church with the enthusiastic proclamation, "I felt the call of God to come here." The people express the same sentiment.

Too many times this beautiful relationship changes. The lovely glow of warmth turns into the white heat of pastor-church frustration, dissatisfaction, and bitterness. The pastor decides he should move. He prays, he puts out "feelers." He waits for that telephone call or letter from an interested pulpit committee. If it does not come when he thinks it should, he becomes overanxious, his work becomes drudgery. He may even think of quitting the ministry. Many pastors will admit that they have passed through phases like this in their ministry.

Is there an answer to a quandary of this kind? Are there Christian principles a pastor can apply in deciding when his work is completed in a specific pastorate? If his church is not ruled by the congregation, others may make the decision for him. If the decision is his, he may discover truth by eliminating the false. He should begin by eliminating some false alarms that sometimes cause pastors to leave:[1]

1. *Apathy among the people.* Too often we become frantic if the people do not respond as we think they should. Sometimes we try to move ahead of the Holy Spirit. We forget that he must take his time to work in the hearts

of the members.

We would gain if at this point we stopped to look in two directions. (1) We should take a good hard look at ourselves. Am I so egotistical that I want the credit? Must I change these people or does God change them through his Spirit? (2) We should look at our people. What is their real nature? What is their background? Am I too far ahead of them or too far behind? Have I tried to drive them or lead them as a shepherd leads his sheep?

One time a young minister faced serious problems on his field of service. In his heart there must have lurked the same apprehension and temptations we often face. Paul wrote him a letter. He did not advise another pastorate. He said, "For this cause left I thee in Crete, that thou shouldst set in order the things that are wanting" (Titus 1:5). The apostle then went on to name some basic qualities a pastor should have. It would do us good to read them again and again.

2. Opposition.   I doubt if any pastor ever served a church three months without some opposition expressed or unexpressed. The devil will see to that. He should remember, however, that opposition to a program he suggests does not necessarily mean opposition to him. Friends can disagree on issues and still be friends.

When opposition to the pastor does arise, he would do well to settle some questions in his mind. Who opposes? How many? For what reason do they oppose? Is the criticism justified? Can this criticism be used to make me a better worker? How Christlike am I under criticism?

Many pastors have run from some opposition only to find more in the new situation. We cannot spend our years running from difficulty. We grow in Christ and retain our self-respect as we learn to deal with opposition.

3. Inadequate salary.   This is a sensitive subject, and it is difficult to determine what an adequate salary should be. The needs of families are different. It is true that a pastor is obliged to support his family. He must do it, and he must pay his obligations. It would follow that he should not accept less that adequate support.

What should he do if he finds after period of time that his salary is not adequate? He cannot afford to start "poor mouthing." Some basic self-questioning is in order. Are my demands reasonable? Does the quality of my work deserve adequate support? Have the people been taught the biblical concept of stewardship? Have I used my salary wisely?

On answering these questions he may find a better solution than moving.

4. Lack of opportunity for family. The pastor should remember that God did his children a favor when he placed them in a minister's home. In spite of the jokes about "preacher's kids," a greater percentage of them succeed than the children of any other profession. Along with some disadvantages there are some distinct advantages.

My wife and I discovered a great truth by experience. Only after we placed our future and the future of our children in the hands of God did doors begin to open. When we could not see, we trusted. It is not a pious platitude when I say he has never failed us.

5. Lack of appreciation. In reply to this alarm, Dr. Hendricks said, "What egotistical fools we pastors can become." Jesus himself was not appreciated by the vast majority. Are we better than our Lord? Of course we love appreciation, but our first goal is to please him who called us. Paul warned, "Let us not be weary in well doing: for in due season we shall reap, if we faint not" (Gal. 6:9). Sometimes we try to reap before we sow. The result is disappointment. The people will usually reward those who serve well. It takes time to earn real appreciation. Remember it must be earned.

6. *Our blunders.* All men are imperfect, and all men make mistakes, even pastors. Our families are not perfect. Our children are not heavenly beings; they are flesh, blood, and bone. A pastor should not be too proud to apologize when he has made a mistake. I have done it, and I have found it drew me closer to my people. Their response was, "Our pastor is human too." Mistakes are a crushing experience if we brood over them. They assume a redemptive purpose if we profit by them. We make another mistake if we run away from them and do not profit from what we have learned.

If the tests we have been discussing are not valid reasons, there must be some that can help us determine when it is time to move on. In most of our experiences, even in a successful pastorate, there comes a time when it is time to move. If we stay very long beyond that time, we might see much of our accomplishment undone. We desire to wear well, but we do not want to wear thin. Surely, there must be some valid tests.

Studying the New Testament, we find Paul making much of what he called "doors." There were "open" and "closed" doors. At one time he wrote a letter from Ephesus to the Corinthian church. He said, "I will tarry at Ephesus until Pentecost. For a great door and effectual is opened unto me" (1 Cor. 16:8,9). His love for his friends and even their need could not tear him away from a door God had opened.

At another time he wanted to go into Asia, but the Holy Spirit did not permit him to preach in Asia (see Acts 16:6). He then tried to go into Bithynia, but the Spirit would not permit it (see Acts 16:7). A. T. Robertson said, "Two rebuffs on the same trip would have discouraged some men." [2] To Paul a closed door meant that God had said, "No." He did not blame his friends. He did not blame the "denomination" down in Jerusalem. He went through the door God had opened to Philippi. God used him to bring revival to that city.

Sometimes we get anxious and overambitious. We try to open doors. The only result is hurt and bruises. As a pastor of some thirty-four years, I admit I have had my anxieties and temptation. I have been discouraged. I have never been called to a place I picked myself. I have wanted some, but they didn't seem to want me. Now as I look back over my ministry, I can honestly say I like the way it turned out. I do not want to live my life over again. I believe the future holds far more exciting adventures. Yet if I were permitted to live my life again and the same churches were to call me, I would gladly go to the same places. The work has not been easy, but it has been rewarding. Never feel let down when God closes a door. He will in his own way open one more effective for you if you are his messenger. It may not be the door of your choosing but if God opened it, it will be better.

Another valid reason is a sense of accomplishment. This is not measured in months or years. A pastor should seriously ask himself, "Have I accomplished the purpose God had in mind for me here?" The work may never be done in a church. We may, however, sense that we have accomplished our part.

I had been pastor of a church for three years. It had not been all happiness. I had inherited some serious problems. The temptation was to leave them for someone else. About that time a young, growing church became interested in me. They seriously asked me to consider being their pastor. I wanted to go. I reasoned, "I have been here longer than the average pastorate lasts. Why not go?" But the more I thought about it, the more I felt it would be a "cop out." Something—or better, *Someone*—seemed to say, "For this cause I sent you." I stayed. I cannot say that my staying saved the church. No great miracles were accomplished. I did see some dreams and hopes come true.

But there's more to that story. A few years after my decision to stay, the same church I had declined issued me a call. This time there were no reservations. I accepted and spent nearly eighteen happy years there. If I had gone the first time, I would never have liked myself. I would have felt guilt about leaving a task unfinished. I do not relate this as an example for others to follow. It may not work that way with you. I do say that some decisions must finally be made in the secret of your own heart. They must be made only between you and your God. He will provide that mysterious guidance of the Spirit.

Another guide that I want to mention could be debatable. Of course different conditions will demand different decisions. I doubt that a pastor should remain if he feels that he can no longer minister effectively to the people. As hostility increases, he may find his own heart growing bitter. If he cannot overcome the bitterness and hostility, it might be better to leave. It might even mean hardship for the pastor and his family. It could even mean a different kind of work. Whatever it means, we cannot afford to use the weapons of the world to fight our battles. That will surely bring defeat. The pastor must be patient, "not a brawler" (1 Tim. 3:3).

I find support for this action in the life of Paul. Some Jews came to Lystra where he was preaching. They stirred up the people. Stones began to fly. After it was over, a blood-splotched body lay outside the city. It looked like the earthly end of Paul. His friends gathered around him and "he rose up" (see Acts 14:20). Paul was no coward. He went back into the city with his friends but the next day he left.

At another time he was asked by some of its leaders to leave a city. We read that "when they had seen the brethren, they comforted them, and departed" (Acts 16:40).

It would be presumptuous to say that a pastor should leave because a few disgruntled people oppose him. They could leave the church as easily as he. It becomes a different matter to him when conditions arise that make it impossible to minister to the people.

Perhaps the most valid test is found in the challenge offered in a new field. When it is clear that the new door offers a better opportunity for you to serve Christ more effectively, it may be time to consider the move. It may not be a larger field or a bigger salary or even the opportunity to baptize more people. The question is: Can you serve Christ more effectively there? I like what a veteran minister said, "I have never been called to a large church, but I left a few."

These reasons coupled with the unexplainable tug of the Holy Spirit may be evidence that one should move.

A further word remains. When it comes time to leave and you know it, leave! It is never wise to threaten to leave. The people just might believe you. They will lose confidence in their pastor if he allows sentiment or personal gain to cause a change of mind. They will wonder if he is close enough to God to know his leading. The greater tragedy is that he himself may lose his sense of direction. God calls us to go forward not backward.

---

1. I am indebted to Dr. Garland A. Hendricks, Southeastern Baptist Seminary, for many of the ideas expressed here. He lectured at the Georgia Baptist Assembly in 1973.

2. A. T. Robertson, *Epochs in the Life of Paul* (New York: Charles Scribner's Sons, 1933), p. 145.

6
Going to
a New Field

In some denominations the placement of pastors is determined by a person or persons other than the local congregation. Such methods have their advantages. They are systematic. A pastor can be reasonably sure that eventually he will have a church. A church can be reasonably sure that it will have a pastor.

Some have said that the weakness of our Baptist denomination is in the area of church-minister relations. We will not argue with that. It may also be true of other autonomous churches. Much grief and heartache has come to pastors and churches in this relationship. We say we try to be led by the Holy Spirit, but the Holy Spirit cannot be charged with everything that happens to our churches in this area.

We may agree that there is a weakness here. But if we look at the structure more closely, we may see that it is our greatest strength. Several points stand out for emphasis: (1) It is democratic. Neither church nor pastor is imposed upon the other. (2) It provides a closer relationship between the pastor and people because the church chose him and he chose them. (3) We feel that it gives better opportunity for guidance of the Holy Spirit. (4) It is more in keeping with the practice and spirit of the New Testament church. (5) It gives an opportunity for longer pastorates.

While democracy may be the most desirable form of government, it is not without its dangers. We must be on our guard against dangers such as the following: (1) Church politics. This monster will show his head in the most holy place. (2) Often weak churches are left pastorless for long periods. (3) Some pastors are tempted to bargain with churches. (4) Churches get divided over pastors. (5) It is more difficult for the younger and older pastors to be called to churches.

What can the pastor do in this type of structure when he feels he should change pastorates?

We might find the right way again by eliminating the wrong. There should never be any "pulling of wires" or "politicking." These methods may seem to work temporarily, but in the long haul they handicap and may destroy.

The pastor will also lose ground if he takes the initiative. Most selection committees will seriously question a man's motive if he contacts them directly, seeking a pastorate. They still feel that the job should seek the man. Pastors should never allow themselves to be in a position of competing with fellow-ministers. They should never bargain for a church.

If these methods are frowned upon by the very nature of our calling, are there others which are scriptural and logical?

It may not be best for him to tell his congregation how he feels. He may later, but not at this point. They may not understand it. He should tell God. He should put himself completely in the will of God. He should not draw a circle around himself and say, "I'll go where you want me to go *within this circle.*" God may have greater things in store for him outside the circle.

He should tell his trusted friends outside his church and ask them to pray with him. It is scriptural and right to do this. God uses human agency to accomplish his purpose now as he did in the past. I have never been called to a church without someone telling them about me.

There is another avenue. Several Baptist state conventions

have, in recent years, set up departments of church-minister relations. These departments cannot solve all our problems, but they are proving helpful. They are not recommending and endorsing agencies. They provide information to churches seeking pastors and to pastors seeking churches. Biographical forms are kept on the pastors and other staff members. This information is shared with churches when they request it.

Usually such an office will provide a church with information about more than one man. This seems to be better for the church and the pastors. The policy guards against partiality and makes it possible to get a man's name before more than one church. After all, *who* can say, "This is where you should go" and "This is the man you should call"? Baptists may tolerate a self-appointed "king maker" for a time, but they do not like it. We believe a denominational office working with the churches can give a wider scope in which the Holy Spirit can work. Do not hesitate to contact your denominational office of church-minister relations. You will find a listening ear and an understanding attitude. But there is a word of caution. Do not expect instant results. God is in this work of changing pastorates. Many lives will be affected by your action. Give the Holy Spirit time to work. Make a progress report from time to time. The office works with many people, and they want to be informed as to your present status. Inform them immediately if you accept a position.

Other denominations have different structures and methods. We all, however, have some of the same experiences when we face a new congregation. There is an element of uncertainty and anxiety. Will the people accept me? Can my children adjust? Will there be the same problems?

We can be sure there *will* be problems. They may have the same nature but different names. We may move our most acute problem with us: *ourselves*. Moving to a new field gives an opportunity to take a new look at yourself and your ministry. Where did I fail? Where did I succeed? What can I do to correct my mistakes? One cannot succeed equally in every field, but too often the man who fails in one fails in another. He is constantly on the move, looking for a better situation and finding none. The answer to his dilemma might be found in evaluating his own work in his last pastorate.

It is important to start right on the new field. Pastorates, like marriages, can be made or marred in the first few months. Many churches have an installation service for the new pastor and his family. This can be very meaningful. However meaningful this formal service is, it will not tie people and pastor together in beautiful relationship. This must come gradually as he ministers to the people in their needs.

One pastor went to a new field with the attitude: "You will serve me." He made many demands of the church. He was a strong pulpiteer, and the people liked that. They thrilled at his preaching. They were proud to say, "Come hear our preacher." They gave him all he asked. Everything went well for a while. It looked like progress, but it didn't last. Praise gave way to bickering. The church began to falter.

Another pastor went to a church with the attitude: "I came to serve you." The people liked that, and they took him literally. It wasn't long before he was "chauffeur-at-large" for the missionary society, caretaker for the church, and general errand boy for the community. The poor man had no time for his family and no time for study or meaningful ministry to those who needed him. The church began to limp.

Another man went to a church with an attitude different

from the other two. He said very frankly, "I did not come for you to serve me. I did not come, primarily, that I might serve you. I came with the purpose of enlisting each member of this church in doing the work of Christ to the best of their ability. I will be in there with you. I will train, guide, encourage, and work, but you will understand it is every Christian's job." I do not need to burden you with words. The church began to grow numerically, spiritually, and financially. A warm relationship grew between pastor and people.

It is important for the pastor to spend the first few months, perhaps the first year, getting acquainted. He needs to know his people, and they need to know him. I heard a renowned pastor say, "No man can remain a great preacher who doesn't visit his people." After being called to a church of over eleven hundred members, I made a list of those who were resident and visited every home. With all my other duties which I did not neglect, it took me eight months. I felt the effort was very worthwhile. Some may find better ways of accomplishing the same results. If there is a better way, use your own plan. The plan is not important. Getting to know your people and having them know you is *very* important.

Out of this knowledge of the people and their needs can come many facets of an effective program for your church. A fringe benefit of knowing and working with your people is support for your program.

Another word of caution may also be in order concerning the program. Of course every effective minister has in his mind some goals he would like to see reached in his church. He needs to know his directions and goals. If he is wise, he will lead his people to make the program, even if it is his, "their program." After all, it is what he can accomplish in and through the church that really matters.

If the program is built around the pastor it will usually fail when he leaves. If it is the program of the church, it will likely continue. There is a fringe benefit in this policy. If the people feel that the program in their church is only the pastor's program, he faces a danger. If they dislike it, they may dislike him. Some will be certain to do it if they feel he has manipulated them to get his idea accepted. If it is their program and they don't like it, they can only blame themselves. They will seek to improve it.

God did not call us to be dictators but to be teachers. He did not call us to drive but to lead.

7
How to
Get Along with
People

Once I asked a fellow minister about a mutual friend. The friend was well-trained, with both college and seminary degrees. He had just completed requirements for his doctorate. Yet his last two pastorates had ended in apparent tragedy. After one year in each, he wanted to leave and his leaders agreed with him. The minister answered my question, "It's the same story here, he just doesn't have *folk-sense.*"

That term made the pastor's point very clear. Most of us could improve our skills in getting along with people. Our knowledge of the Bible, our new educational methods, even our sincerity of character will be handicapped if we cannot work with people. To say the right thing at the wrong time may create as much damage as saying the wrong thing. It is as important to know when to listen as it is to know when to talk. The pastor may be king in the pulpit, but he should be a good listener to his people during the week. There are many truths he can hear from *them.*

Our greatest teacher in this area is Jesus. If the great works on psychology, diplomacy, and interpersonal relationships were condensed to a few short pages, we would probably find something like the Sermon on the Mount. As we study Jesus' contacts with individuals, we can discover some guiding principles which are timeless.

1. He looked for something good in people. When the sinful woman washed his feet with her tears and dried them with her hair, he justified her before the critical and sophis-

ticated guests in the house of Simon the Pharisee (Luke 7:36-50). He did not at first point to her sins which were many. He looked for and found some good. He complimented her actions. This opened the way for her to recognize and receive forgiveness of sins.

2. He was kind to people, even the unlovely. Not many people in Jericho would have been seen with Zacchaeus. No Jew would have been caught eating in his house. Yet Jesus said, "Zacchaeus, make haste, and come down; for to day I must abide at thy house" (Luke 19:5). Kindness melts the ice of hostility. The cold winds of criticism only solidify it.

3. He began with people where they were and recognized their present interests. He made conversation with the Samaritan woman about her humdrum household chores, like drawing water from the well. This led easily to her deep spiritual needs. Had he bluntly told her of her failures, he would have built a judgmental wall between her and himself. Jesus always faced up to the facts of life. Too often the pastor cannot accept people as they are. He must accept them as they are as persons before he can lead them to where they ought to be.

4. Jesus let people make their own decisions. He did not manipulate them. You remember the case of the rich young ruler (Luke 18:18-24). Jesus gave him the facts, but he did not coerce him. He always went so far with people and then left them to make their own decisions. If he stormed our wills and crushed them, he would not save us. He would destroy a vital part of us. The Christian leader can learn a lesson from the Master. We are not to force our wills upon people even if we are right.

5. Jesus respected the identity of people. He often spoke to masses of people, but he did not see them as masses or congregations but as individuals. He did not try to force

them into the same mold. Dictators and tyrants do that. It is essential in communism and fascism, but it is contrary to Christianity. Peter, James, and John loved and followed the same Christ, but they did not lose their identities. Christ used their different personalities and talents for their good and his glory. The pastor may be thrilled by his large congregation, but he will not be effective until he sees them as individuals.

This method of Jesus can be put to effective use by the pastor in his relationship with his people. "Let this mind be in you, which was also in Christ Jesus" (Phil. 2:5).

The pastor who builds or inherits a staff in his church will find an area where he can use all he knows about interpersonal relationship. It can become a very sensitive area. Trouble with a staff member can be almost as grievous as trouble with one's wife. We believe that the principles Jesus used will also work with staff members as well as others. In addition to these principles, there are some specifics that have worked in many instances.

It is always good to have the areas of work defined. To call a staff member and only say, "You know what you are supposed to do," can invite trouble. Of course a job description can be too legalistic, but the area of work should be defined. If fringe benefits, such as time for vacation, sick leave, convention expenses, housing, and travel, are defined in the beginning, that can save misunderstanding later on. In the case of associate pastors, the associate should be told his duties. If he is expected to preach, baptize, etc., at the option of the pastor, it should be made clear to him. The associate should not try to step beyond his assigned duties. Although the entire staff looks to the pastor for guidance, the pastor should allow each one to use and develop his own talents. After all, that is the real reason for calling them. The call is wasted if they are not permitted to use and develop their talents.

Lines of communication should be kept open. When they are not open something has to give. If the deadlock continues, usually the pastor and staff pay the penalty. All suffer.

When I was a pastor, we had a set time each week for a staff meeting. Each person was given the opportunity to voice his ideas, fears, frustrations, expectations, and disappointments. This was not a waste of time. It saved time. We would get together at other times if emergencies arose. We had a gentleman's agreement that none of us would introduce a new program of any significance until we had all agreed upon it or at least agreed not to oppose it. I feel this is wise. If the staff is divided, the church will usually be divided in about the same proportion.

In addition to these guidelines, *there must be Christian love and respect among members of the staff.* This doesn't always come easy. Each member must work at it. The same principles apply here as they do in the home. No one hands you a happy home prepaid. You must build it. The right sort of staff relationships must be built. There is no room for distrust and jealousy. The pastor should feel complimented when someone compliments a member of his staff. The staff members should feel complimented when someone compliments his pastor. If we are willing to share responsibility, we should also be willing to share honors and glory. Much of the friction among staff members is due to a lack of these virtues.

Some pastors are given unlimited authority by their churches to hire and fire staff members. The reasoning is that the church looks to the pastor for leadership and therefore the staff should be in complete harmony with him. Of course it is desirable that the pastor and staff be in harmony, but I doubt the wisdom of arrangements like this. Even if a staff member becomes incorrigible and is fired, the problem is not solved for the pastor. The incorrigible staff member will have friends who can become thorns in the flesh of the pastor.

It seems that in a democratic institution like a church, *the better plan would be to have a personnel committee.* This committee could serve as arbitrators in differences among staff members and could make recommendations to the church when such a course is needed. This could tend to keep matters from developing into personal issues between the pastor and staff.

Another area of concern with some pastors is relationship with former pastors. This relationship should concern us all because sooner or later we will be former pastors. The difficulties grow out of the unique relationship between pastor and people. It is more personal than the relationship between attorney and client or physician and patient.

For this cause it is often a traumatic experience for both pastor and people to break the ties. In fact, all ties should not be broken. The ties of friendship should remain. The former pastor should retain his interest in the spiritual welfare of the members he has taught and led to Christ. He should not, however, allow himself to become a problem for the new pastor. He can prevent this if he tries.

I have known instances where a retired minister remained on the field and became a source of strength to the new pastor. This is not always the case. The success of this arrangement may depend upon circumstances and the personalities of those involved. Usually it is best to leave when one resigns.

Occasionally, it will be necessary and wise for the former pastor to return for some service. If this happens, it should be with the knowledge and consent of the present pastor. The former pastor should never do or say anything that would cast reflection upon the present pastor.

The present pastor also has an obligation. He should respect what has been done before he came on the scene. He should never allow himself to make derogatory remarks about the former pastor. It may be wise for him to counsel with him concerning what has been done. It is difficult to chart the future without knowing the past.

When the former pastor returns to the field, he should be shown warm Christian courtesy. The people are quick to detect any sign of jealousy. God's pulpit servants should conquer this sin.

If the former pastor does cause trouble, it will not help you to fight him. The word to use here is *love*. You can "handle" him with love. I have found that the people who are loyal to one pastor in a church will usually be loyal to another. I have also found that the closest friends, that is true friends, of the former pastors sooner or later became my friends.

When we come to see that God called us to perform special phases of his ministry, our problem diminishes. When we get God in proper focus there is no problem. Paul gave the answer: "I have planted, Apollos watered; but God gave the increase" (1 Cor. 3:6).

8
Power
Structures

Gaines Dobbins, beloved and honored professor at both Southern and Golden Gate seminaries, sometimes applied the case-study method to pastors' problems. He described the "church boss" as one who was especially fond of his prerogative in virtually selecting the new pastor and saw to it that he was given this opportunity frequently.[1] He exercised this prerogative about every two years. The new pastor accepted the church ignorant of its past history. He proposed an aggressive program. He soon found himself opposed, bullied, and insulted by this dignified, pompous, self-appointed "church boss." He had enough influence to carry the vote. What should a pastor do, fight to the finish or resign?

Some churches develop what is often labeled power structures. Sometimes they grow up around a person like, or unlike, the one described above. They can be built around a family, a particular doctrine, or some event in the history of the church. They may take the form of youth and adult groups struggling for control.

They may lie dormant for years but rise up in fury if they are aroused. In fairness to them, we must say they are not all bad, but they are potentially dangerous. We are tempted to consider them bad if they oppose us, and good if they are going our way. Whether they oppose us or work for us, they are bad if they obstruct the work of the church as a whole.

A pastor can be the worst offender in building power

structures if he chooses to do so. Of course, he would not call his actions politics. He might assume a holy air and label them divine strategies. Whatever he calls them, the end result is usually the same—cliques and confusion in the church and trouble for the pastor.

If a pastor is tempted to control people in this manner, he should remember that his profession is a unique calling. He is not the president of a corporation or the head of a political party. He is the "under shepherd" of a flock. The most effective way is to teach, preach, and lead. If he gets too far ahead of his people, they will not hear him. If he gets behind them, they will lose him.

Just voting a program through does not spell success. Unless we carry the people with us, we have not accomplished much. If we patiently give the people the truth, they will generally do right. Prayer, loving concern, and teaching are stronger weapons than voting and confrontation. It sometimes takes more courage to follow this course than to thunder like an Amos.

Once a church was in bitter conflict over its pastor. Both sides were urged to wait and give God a chance to work. They wanted to vote, to have a confrontation. (You can always do that in like circumstance, but like war, it doesn't always settle problems.) After prayer, both sides decided to wait from three to six months. In less than three months the problem was settled. They learned that no church is ready to vote on disturbing issues until the people have sought and found God's will.

But the pastor is not always at fault when power structures arise. What is the best course to follow when faced with a struggle in the church that threatens destruction? Shall he join the long list of "resigners" or risk his future in a fight to the finish? Of course there is no easy answer and no standard answer for every occasion. Each situation will be different. The wisest course may be found in refusing to resign or to fight.

Two good words to consider are *time* and *patience.* Time has a way of rectifying many wrongs. Rome was not built in a day, and Nero did not become a tyrant overnight. Evil power structures do not usually form suddenly. They do not normally disappear with the wave of a hand. The pastor should keep these facts in mind when his patience begins to waver.

One modern Christian leader, when faced by a hostile power structure, said, "Those who believe in God can afford to wait." I have always felt that there is a workable, right solution to every problem. Our job is to find it. The pessimist will say after he has tried and tried and tried, "I can't do it. I will quit." The optimist will say, "I have found certain ways it can't be done, now I will find the right way." Edison worked on that principle and finally invented the light bulb. The Christian worker can profit from his experience.

Sometimes troublesome power structures can be overcome by the infusion of new blood into the congregation. Sick churches, like sick bodies, sometimes need a transfusion of healthy blood. New members coming in will add new enthusiasm and fresh ideas. A pastor once said, "I have found if we can keep the water rising, the deadwood will float off to the side, out of the main stream."

The pastor should not forget that he is working with families and individuals. They do not look alike, and they do not think alike. They do not all behave alike. All this means that problems will continue to arise. That was true in the early church. "There arose a murmuring of the Grecians against the Hebrews" (Acts 6:1). The twelve found themselves in the crossfire. It was not cowardice but wisdom that prompted them to lay the burden upon the church. Sometimes pastors try to carry too much of the burden.

One cold rainy day a pastor called to say he must talk with someone. He came through forty miles of rain to share his problem with a fellow pastor. The problem was a power struggle rooted in a legalistic interpretation of Scripture. It could lead and was leading to a serious rupture in the fellowship. A very vocal but weak minority seemed determined to pull the church away from its denominational ties. The pastor was asked if he had shared his fear and anxieties with his trusted church leaders. He had not. He agreed to do that, and he did. Sometime later he reported, "After I brought the laymen into it, things got worse but *now* they are getting better." When a pastor is right, the sincere laymen will do a better job of defending him than he can do himself. They will enjoy doing it.

Sometimes we are tempted to make great issues out of minor problems because they irritate us or wound our pride. Before a pastor stakes his ministry on an issue, he should be sure it involves a basic principle. For example, methods are important, but they are not principles. We may compromise on most methods but not on principles.

Because he is called of God, sometimes a pastor must take the stance of a prophet. Like Elijah he must ask, "How long halt ye between two opinions?" He must declare, "If the Lord be God, follow him: but if Baal then follow him" (1 Kings 18:21). Like Nathan he must say to enthroned evil, "Thou art the man" (2 Sam. 12:7). Like his Lord he must "steadfastly set his face to go to Jerusalem" (Luke 9:51).

When such time comes, the true minister will not think primarily of self or rules of personal relationship. His first purpose will be to be true to God and the convictions of his heart.

He must also be prepared to pay the price of a prophet. That price has always been high on the world's market. It is no different today. The world does not treat prophets kindly.

The prophet has his rewards, however, and they are lasting. He has the heart-warming assurance of the presence of the Lord. He has the certainty of ultimate victory. Truth is stronger than error. It will ultimately triumph. When a man is walking with God, he may suffer; he may experience temporary defeat but nothing will finally stop him. Our chief concern is to find the direction God is moving and move with him.

1. Gaines S. Dobbins, *Building Better Churches* (Nashville: Broadman Press, 1947), p. 415.

9
Land Mines to Avoid

One Sunday morning a young man rolled down the aisle in a wheelchair to confess Christ as Savior. The pastor knew his story. He was a war veteran. He had stepped on a land mine in Korea. He was a victim of the cruelty of war. His confession thrilled the pastor and audience. He became an esteemed member of the church, and he served Christ in many ways. Because of the loss of his legs, however, his activity was curtailed as long as he lived.

The pastor is ever aware that an even more cruel war is being waged in the moral and spiritual realm. Peter was aware of the dangers facing every Christian. He said, "Be sober, be vigilant; because your adversary the devil, as a roaring lion, walketh about, seeking whom he may devour" (1 Pet. 5:8).

The pastor and other staff members are not shielded from this danger. Whatever idea you may have of the devil, you will find his power very real. Billy Sunday was quoted as saying, "I know there is a devil because I have done business with him." Most of us to our sorrow must admit that we have had similar experiences. His ways are sometimes subtle. He plants devastating, sometimes hidden mines in our paths. We do not like to talk of these subjects or even think of them, but they are real dangers. Too often we read or hear of some pastor or staff member who leaves his church under a cloud. God may forgive, but too often he is permanently injured. His effectiveness is curtailed, and the cause of Christ suffers as well as those who are near and dear.

One of the land mines could be labeled impurity. It is not, however, so labeled. Sometimes it comes in a beautiful, almost holy, setting. The pastor has many privileges. Both men and women come to him for counsel and guidance. Sometimes it is easy for him to become personally involved. The very moment he begins to feel he is too personally involved in a relationship with one of the opposite sex, he should change that relationship. I firmly believe that if a pastor conducts himself as a pastor should, he will not be bothered by advances on the part of even unchristian women. It takes two to play that game. This does not mean he must be a prude. I knew one pastor who wouldn't even shake hands with the sisters! That's going too far. It is also going too far when it becomes a game—playing hands. Too many pastors have allowed a Christian friendship to become an "affair." As a result their churches, their families, and they have suffered. One never fully recovers from such an experience. The crippling effect continues.

There is one effective defense against this danger available to every Christian worker. Joseph found it in the long ago. He had a bracing sense of God. This support enabled him to say, "How then can I do this great wickedness, and sin against God?" (Gen. 39:9). He fixed his gaze not on the temptress—or the tempter within himself—but on his Deliverer. This brought victory. We have available the same source of strength. Paul put the answer very plainly. We need to heed it again and again. "This I say then, Walk in the Spirit, and ye shall not fulfill the lust of the flesh" (Gal. 5:16).

Another mine fixed by Satan looks innocent enough. It is hidden in the area of finance. It appeals to our primitive instinct. We all have a desire to possess, to accumulate. It is a legitimate desire. Out of it comes progress and many problems. Jesus recognized this hunger in man's heart. Out of it came many of his most exciting stories. He spoke of hidden treasures, pearls of great price, coins of value. Like any other instinct, it becomes a sin when diverted from its original intent.

Tolstoy illustrated this sin with a story about the man who was land-hungry. He was given a promise that he could have all the land he could walk around from sunrise to sunset. At the first blush of dawn he started out leisurely enough. Then the black soil took on the luster of gold. He quickened his pace so that he could encircle more land. He went farther and faster. One word burned in his heart and soul, "More!" As the sun began to set, he went faster and faster forcing his body beyond its endurance. Finally with a mighty surge he flung himself forward touching the goal and dropped there—dead! There they buried him in his soil.

Most pastors do not have this insatiable desire for material wealth. If they did, they would not have surrendered to the call of the ministry. There are, however, some hidden dangers.

We live in a time of easy credit. The temptation is to buy whether we can pay or not. It is so easy to stamp a credit card and promise to pay later. Many pastors have fallen into Satan's trap here.

Someone told of a young pastor and his wife who fell into serious financial difficulty. They held a family council. They agreed that neither one would make a purchase above five dollars without consulting the other. The young wife had a weakness for pretty clothes. One day while casually walking through a department store, she saw a dress she couldn't resist. She bought it and charged it.

When the husband came home that night, she had it on. He stopped and stood speechless. Finally, wringing his hands, he said, "But I told you. I told you, and we agreed!" She said, "But the devil tempted me." The husband asked, "Why didn't you say, 'Get thee behind me, Satan'?" She said, "I did but he slipped around me to my back and whispered in my ear, 'It looks prettier in the back than the front.'"

We are all tempted to spend beyond our means in a country where there is so much to buy. We cannot afford to buy at the expense of our good name. It is more honorable to do without than to default on a debt. When a pastor fails to pay his bills, he loses the respect of laymen. It is true that he must care for his family and his own needs. He must also pay his debts. A good name down at the bank is as good a recommendation in the eyes of a pastor selection committee as a letter from the president of a theological seminary. It is far better if one can have both.

Sometimes certain people will take advantage of the pastor's sympathy by asking him to be surety for their debts. The wise pastor will exercise caution here. Most honest people will not take advantage of a pastor in this way. It is usually better to make a gift of what you can afford in cash rather than sign notes. You can easily bring yourself to grief. Some of us have learned that the hard way.

The pastor will find that another subtle danger lies in the very nature of his calling. He has no boss. He is not generally given a job description. There are no set hours, except his regular hours of worship and other church meetings. To the casual observer it may look like a soft job.

The experienced pastor knows differently. He can either work himself to death or he can become "hound dog" lazy.

If he chooses the former route, he may experience a heart attack by the time he is forty. He may also face serious emotional disturbances and nervous disorders. We may be strong but we live in mortal bodies. All of us have a breaking point. Some of the danger signals are insomnia and inability to relax. The church is wise that insists on its pastor taking *a day of rest* each week. The pastor will be wise to accept it. Weddings and funerals may barge in to take priority, but he should try to shift to another day. A deacon told his pastor that he should not take a vacation. He said, "The devil is always on the job and the pastor should be." The pastor replied, "But I'm not the devil. I am made out of flesh and blood and, besides, I do not want to pattern my life after him."

If the pastor so chooses, he may neglect his work. Golf and fishing have therapeutic values. If carried to extremes, they become a killing disease. The pastor who fails to discipline himself to regular hours for study, visitation, and administrative duties will soon find himself wearing thin with the people. They know as well as he when he is not prepared. His youth and enthusiasm may carry him for a while. People are sympathetic with a novice, but this attitude will not go on forever. He cannot continue just as a brilliant young man. He must accomplish something. Jesus set the example. He said, "My Father worketh hitherto, and I work" (John 5:17). There is no substitute for hard work.

A mine skillfully placed and sometimes coated with slick piosity is the neglect of one's family. We are constantly stressing commitment and loyalty. We feel an obligation to the church program. Our work is like a woman's housework; it is never done. We are urged to put our church first. We feel irreligious when we don't. Feelings of guilt pile up.

Of course God should come first in a pastor's life. He should be first in every life. That relationship is established at conversion and reaffirmed in our call. The same God who commands this relationship with us gave us some priorities. He established the institution of home before he established the church. If the pastor spends his time in church duties and neglects his wife and the parental training of his children, he grieves God and sins against him. The sin will eventually catch up with him. Paul felt so keenly about it that he wrote to young Timothy: "But if any provide not for his own, and specially for those of his own house, he hath denied the faith, and is worse than an infidel" (1 Tim. 5:8). The apostle must have intended us to do more than provide food, clothing, and shelter. I read in the command the necessity of providing companionship, love, and spiritual guidance. The pastor who neglects this may gain professional eminence among his peers, but he will lose joy and satisfaction that comes to a godly parent and husband. His effectiveness as a minister may finally be impaired.

10
The
Home Stretch

Some retired ministers got together at a state convention for a banquet. They were having informal discussions about their work since retirement. Some told of their interim pastorates, revivals, Bible classes, and other projects. One man rose to say that he had moved to a community, joined a small church, and was finding fulfillment in being an active member there.

Get any group of retired ministers together, and you will hear them talking of work or their desire to work. Recently our state denominational magazine asked all retired ministers to send their names, addresses, telephone numbers, and the type of service they felt prepared to do. The idea was to publish these names and make a file of them in the office of Church-Minister Relations Service. It was hoped to refer this information to the churches when they needed it. We were amazed at the number of responses. We learned that ministers are not satisfied to fish, hunt, play golf, and just plain loaf after they retire. You can quit a job, but not a calling. With apology to Robert Frost, we would say "something there is" about a true minister that doesn't like a rocking chair. That "something" may have its roots in the "tap on the shoulder" that came from God.

In his middle forties, busy preparing sermons, conducting funerals, officiating at weddings, counseling the troubled, visiting the sick, administering the organizations, he may long for retirement. Many do. When that day comes, he will probably face it with mixed emotions. One man said,

"The hardest road I ever traveled was from my house to my office on the day of retirement." Yet the day will come for most of us when we must at least shift gears.

It can be a devastating experience if we are not prepared for it. It can be a new exciting adventure if we have laid the right foundation. Preparation for this experience should be started at the beginning of one's ministry. Financial preparation is important, but it is not enough. We need to be prepared spiritually, mentally, and physically.

Our spiritual outlook is important. The letter to the Hebrews will be found spiritually rewarding to the minister. It was addressed to a group of Hebrews who had accepted Christianity at great cost to themselves. The letter has many purposes, but the chief purpose was to save them from a backward step. The writer called their attention to the better things they had received; better revelation, better country, better faith, better future. As if he were talking to us personally he wrote, "So we must listen very carefully to the truths we have heard, or we may drift away from them" (Heb. 2:1, TLB).[1] At no time can a minister neglect his spiritual life. He can drift backward at eighty as well as twenty. As he nears the sunset years, he will need to draw more and more from the deep wells of his Christian faith.

Health is important, but old age and poor health do not necessarily have to go together. Poor health does not automatically descend upon us at a certain age. God made us to live longer and more successfully than most of us will. We hinder his blessings by disregarding the simple laws of health. Observing good health habits and adjusting to the emotional and psychological pressures of retirement will bring happy rewards. It will pay dividends to go to your physician for regular check-ups even if you feel fine. We should at least give our bodies as much care as we do our automobiles if we expect efficient performance.

Financial security has always been a problem for ministers. Although the conditions have improved, some laymen still like to help the Lord "keep the pastor humble by keeping him poor, so that he will be more spiritual." No man in his right mind would enter the ministry with the sole purpose of making money. He can, however, by observing sound financial principles, provide for himself, his family, and his retirement. He can and should practice the biblical concept of stewardship. He will need to start this discipline at the beginning of his ministry.

The only way to save money is to spend less than you make and do it regularly. Two problems emerge here for the minister. Inflation has tended to eat up savings in recent years. There are also few times in the minister's life when he can meet all his financial demands and save regularly.

One possible answer is to buy a house. Many churches will gladly give their pastor a housing allowance in lieu of a pastorium provided by the church. In our recent economy, this provision has held some definite advantage for the pastor. It is tax-sheltered, and it generally provides a safe way to build an equity. It will give a sense of security when one nears retirement if he has a place he can call his own.

Most denominations in recent years have provided an annuity plan for pastors and other staff members. Many churches pay both the pastor's dues and that of the church. The church will be acting wise to do this if it can. The pastor will be wise if early in his ministry he investigates and enters the retirement plans of his denomination. They were built with him and his financial security in mind. It is also good sense and good religion to carry adequate health and life insurance.

Even if the minister has reasonable financial security and

a measure of health, he will not be satisfied just to live. What can he do? There are some "no-no's." He cannot meddle in the affairs of his former church. He must be careful lest he become a problem in the church he joins. The pastor who welcomes him to his congregation will not look kindly upon his unsolicited advice or well-meaning meddling. He will not want to continually hear how you did things in your own church. This will call for an adjustment in your role.

Life, however, need not be empty and meaningless. There will always be Christian work for those who are able, willing, and consecrated. Some will be limited in activity because of health or other problems. Perhaps that day may come to all of us. If it does I hope I can share the attitude of Paul. He wrote, "Now I have given up everything else—I have found it to be the only way to really know Christ and to experience the mighty power that brought him back to life again and to find out what it means to suffer and to die with him" (Phil. 3:10, TLB). There is a ministry in suffering.

Other ministers will find new avenues. New doors of opportunity will open for them. Some will be kept busy in supply work and interim pastorates. Some pastors have done their most effective work after retirement in this ministry to churches in crisis. Sometimes an idea has lain long and dormant in your mind. You wanted to put it into writing but you never had time. You may find that time in retirement. There is always the opportunity to witness. Witnessing is not something you go and do. It is something you do as you go. That kind is most effective. If we but look we will never find time to do all the good things we see that need to be done.

The married minister should also remember that retirement brings changes and adjustments for his wife. For years she has been at the center of the stage. Now she is sometimes in the wings. In a way, she and her husband are just two more members of the church. Her answer to her problem is much the same as that of her husband. She must seek out the new advantages that have come to her and assume new responsibilities in the new role. Perhaps in her new freedom she can find opportunities to develop skills that have lain dormant and make new friends. There is no reason why one cannot keep learning and growing in mental and spiritual stature. In retirement a couple may find the richest companionship of their married life. Real life does not begin at forty. It can begin every day.

Finally—and we don't like that word. There is a thud about it that sounds unchristian. We use it only in reference to time. Finally, we must lay down our earthly tools and enter the door to a larger realm and a fuller life. Some people say they are not interested in the future life, only the present world. They speak contemptuously of "pie in the sky by and by." It is the voice of impatient youth, not maturity. We can use our "pie" now, and we need it. It will be nice to have it in "the sky by and by." I expect to spend more time there than I have spent here.

In an interview just before his death, Bishop Arthur Moore, who was then 85, said, "I'm ready to die, not in any boastful sort of way, but because I am an ardent believer in personal and instant immortality. I don't believe God can be good and kind and merciful to someone who has served him faithfully and just let death cut off all that communion and let you drop into oblivion. I like to believe even after I die the Lord will find something to be done with me to help here on earth." [2] I believe he will.

---

1. *The Living Bible, Paraphrased.* © Tyndale House Publishers, 1971. Used by permission.

2. *Atlanta Constitution*, July 1, 1974.